FACT FRENZY

PLANET EARTH

MOUNTAINS AND RIVERS

Lisa Regan

PowerKiDS press

Published in 2020 by **The Rosen Publishing Group, Inc.**
29 East 21st Street, New York, NY 10010

Cataloging-in-Publication Data

Names: Regan, Lisa.
Title: Mountains and rivers / Lisa Regan.
Description: New York : PowerKids Press, 2020. | Series: Fact frenzy: planet Earth | Includes glossary and index.
Identifiers: ISBN 9781725395596 (pbk.) | ISBN 9781725395619 (library bound) | ISBN 9781725395602 (6 pack)
Subjects: LCSH: Mountains--Juvenile literature. | Rivers--Juvenile literature.
Classification: LCC GB512.R43 2020 | DDC 551.43'2--dc23

Manufactured in the United States of America

CPSIA Compliance Information: Batch CSPK20: For Further Information contact Rosen Publishing, New York, New York at 1-800-237-9932.

Contents

FACT 1 ROCKS CAN BE FOLDED

The world's biggest mountain ranges are made of rocks that have been crushed and folded. The Himalayas, Alps, and Andes are all fold mountains. Smaller rocks can also be folded under pressure, creating spectacular visual effects.

Around the world

Fold mountains are the most common type of mountain. They are found all over the world: the Rockies and Appalachians in the U.S., the Urals between Europe and Asia, Australia's Great Dividing Range, and the Atlas mountains in Africa are other examples. Some were formed over 200 million years ago, while others are relatively young ranges, only 10 to 25 million years old. These younger mountains tend to be more rugged, with high peaks, as they have not been subjected to so many millennia of erosion.

FACT 2

New Zealand's Southern Alps are young mountains and did not exist until 5 million years ago.

Making a mountain

Most fold mountains are found on the edge of a plate boundary. The rock layers are pushed upward as two convergent plates crash into each other. The rocks at the edge of a plate are often weaker than those in the interior, making it easier for them to be squeezed and folded over one another. It is much the same as a car crash: two vehicles colliding with each other will crumple and bend.

FACT 3 Mountain ranges can link together to form a long chain known as a cordillera.

Steep and high

Mountains can also form at faults or cracks in Earth's crust. Some sections of the crust collapse inward and down, while others are pushed up in enormous blocks that form sheer, steep rock faces. The Sierra Nevada range in the U.S. is a spectacular example of steep, cliff-like mountains. It contains Mount Whitney, the highest peak in the contiguous U.S.

Up and down

Mountains are constantly changing landforms. Erosion wears away the rocks and gravity carries the particles down the slopes. A huge landslide in 1991 caused Mount Cook in New Zealand to shrink by 33 feet (10 m). However, many mountains are growing slightly bigger, as the forces pushing them together continue to act on them. The Himalayas are already huge, and are growing by around 0.75 inch (20 mm) each year.

THE MATTERHORN IS A FOLD MOUNTAIN THAT HAS BEEN ERODED BY GLACIERS.

FACT 4 EVEREST IS NOT OUR TALLEST MOUNTAIN

The Himalayas contain 10 of the world's 14 highest peaks, including Everest. But some of the world's tallest mountains would dwarf those peaks if the ocean wasn't covering them.

ANYTHING OVER 2,000 FEET (610 M) IS CLASSIFIED AS A MOUNTAIN.

Tallest or highest?

A mountain can be measured from sea level to its peak. In that way, Everest is the highest, at just over 29,000 feet (8,850 m). However, mountains such as Mauna Kea, in Hawaii, are partially hidden underwater. Measured from its base to its peak, Mauna Kea is 33,374 feet (10,203 m), making it taller but not actually higher. Its height above sea level is only 13, 796 feet (4,205 m)—less than half the height it would need to be the world's highest.

The peaks of volcanoes poke out of the water as islands.

Bubbling under

The longest mountain range on Earth is mostly hidden under the ocean. It stretches from the Arctic Ocean down to the South Atlantic for over 10,000 miles (16,000 km) and consists of strings of volcanoes. Underwater volcanoes are formed in the same way as they are on land, by the Earth's plates moving and allowing hot rocks to rise up through a gap. Around 90 percent of the mid-Atlantic ridge is hidden underwater.

THE HIGHEST MOUNTAIN IN THE SOLAR SYSTEM IS OLYMPUS MONS ON MARS, OVER TWICE THE HEIGHT OF EVEREST.

Reach for the moon

There is a third mountain on Earth that can stake a claim to the title of tallest: Mount Chimborazo in Ecuador. It is not the highest above sea level, but because of the bulge of our planet around the equator, Chimborazo's summit is the farthest point from the middle of Earth. It is also the point on Earth's surface that is the closest to the moon!

Head for heights

There are 14 mountains that reach over 26,247 feet (8,000 m) above sea level, and they form an elite list for mountaineers wishing to climb them. All of them are in Asia. The "eight-thousanders" all have summits in the death zone, where there is too little oxygen to breathe without help.

FACT 5 MOUNTAIN CLIMBING IS BANNED IN BHUTAN

Bhutan is a small country in the Himalayas and contains several high peaks, but no mountaineering has been allowed there since 2003. Hikers are prevented from going above around 13,000 feet (4,000 m).

OVER 4,000 PEOPLE HAVE CLIMBED EVEREST, BUT MORE THAN 290 PEOPLE HAVE DIED TRYING.

No-go zone

Many of Bhutan's peaks are considered sacred, and the Bhutanese government prohibited the climbing of them out of respect. Additionally, there are no rescue teams to help people in case of an emergency. Mountain climbing is a dangerous activity, and peaks in most countries have search-and-rescue teams close by if climbing parties get stuck. In 1996, eight people died in one day attempting to climb Everest; as a consequence, safety measures were drastically improved.

South African Bernard Goosen climbed Kilimanjaro in a wheelchair—twice!

Seven summits

The first person to climb the highest mountain on each of the seven continents was an American, Richard Bass, in 1985. Everest is, of course, the highest and ticks Asia off the list. Australia's Mount Kosciuszko is the smallest of the seven. The easiest to climb is Africa's Mount Kilimanjaro, and its summit can be reached just by hiking.

The high life

Life in the mountains can be tough. Mountaineers often carry their own oxygen as it becomes harder to breathe at altitude. Around 2 percent of the world's population lives permanently in these conditions. Scientists have found that the bodies of people living in the Andes, the Himalayas, and Ethiopia have adapted to cope better with breathing this "thin" air.

KILIMANJARO HAS GLACIERS ON TOP EVEN THOUGH IT IS NEAR THE EQUATOR.

On top of the world

Many animals have also adapted to live in low-oxygen environments. There is as little as 40 percent of the oxygen high in the mountains, and animals such as llamas have more red blood cells, allowing their blood to react better with the limited oxygen. Llamas and mountain goats have feet that give them the best possible grip on uneven, rocky ground.

FACT 6 YOU DRINK THE SAME WATER DINOSAURS DRANK!

The planet has a limited amount of water that is constantly recycled. It is the same water that the dinosaurs drank, and it will still be here millions of years into the future.

RAINDROPS ARE SPHERICAL AT FIRST AND THEN TAKE THE SHAPE OF A JELLY BEAN.

Around and around

This constant flow of water is known as the water cycle. Water enters the atmosphere in its gaseous form, and condenses as it cools, forming raindrops. These fall to Earth and the water collects in puddles, rivers, lakes, and the ocean. It evaporates again, entering the atmosphere, and the process repeats itself endlessly. Of course, the water can be diverted and used for drinking, sanitation, irrigation, or manufacturing, but ultimately it keeps its place in the water cycle.

Into the air

Liquid water gets into the air by evaporation and also by transpiration. With evaporation, heat energy turns the water from a liquid into a gas and it rises upward before cooling again to form clouds. Transpiration takes place when plants pull water up from the ground and release it through their leaves. A single corn plant loses nearly 0.5 gallon (2 l) of water per day, which is over 52 gallons (200 l) in one growing season.

Rain or shine?

There is water in the air even on a cloudless day. It sits in tiny droplets that are too small to see. Once these combine with tiny particles of dust or smoke, they gather and grow into clouds. There are ten basic cloud types, varying from high, wispy cirrus clouds made of ice crystals to giant, anvil-shaped cumulonimbus clouds that bring very heavy rain.

A RAINDROP CAN SPEND TEN DAYS IN THE SKY BEFORE IT FALLS.

Acid rain

Clearly, the type of water that evaporates will affect the rain that eventually falls. Unpolluted rainwater is slightly acidic, with a pH of about 5.6. The rain that falls in parts of Costa Rica has a pH of 2 or lower, which is extremely strong acid. It has evaporated from the Laguna Caliente, a volcanic lake which sometimes even blasts out its acidic water as a geyser.

Laguna Caliente is on top of the still-active Poás Volcano.

FACT 7 THE HUDSON RIVER FLOWS IN TWO DIRECTIONS

Its Native American name means "river that flows two ways." It begins by flowing south near its source (the Adirondack Mountains in New York State) and then, near the Atlantic, it swaps and flows north with the tide.

Back and forth

Most rivers work their way downhill until they reach the coast at the river mouth. Some rivers flow into a lake or another river. Rivers that have their mouth at the ocean may be affected by the tides, with water flowing back upriver at high tide. The Hudson River is unusual as it has an extremely long (153 miles/246 km) estuary, so nearly half of its length is affected by tides.

THE SEVEN SPIKES ON THE STATUE OF LIBERTY'S CROWN REPRESENT THE SEVEN CONTINENTS.

Meeting the ocean

An estuary is an area where a freshwater river meets the salt water of the ocean. It can create a unique ecosystem, inhabited by creatures and plants that can survive in brackish (partly salty) water. Some rivers form wide deltas as they slow down in their lower stages and deposit any sediment that has been carried along. The soil in a delta is usually very fertile.

Starting point

The beginning of a river is called its source. It may start as a small mountain stream or spring, a melting glacier, or an outlet from a lake. Other streams and rivers, called tributaries, might join along the way. The world's longest river, the Nile, has two main tributaries that flow from lakes in different countries. It finally meets the Mediterranean Sea after flowing for 4,145 miles (6,670 km) through ten countries.

Who lives here?

Rivers provide a home for a huge variety of freshwater wildlife, including fish, birds, amphibians, and mammals. Bull sharks are notorious for leaving the ocean and swimming far upriver. River dolphins used to live in some of the world's largest rivers but are struggling to survive among heavy boat traffic and in polluted water.

Pink dolphins live in the Amazon and, unlike sea dolphins, have a flexible neck.

FACT 8

The Nile is long enough to flow across the U.S., from New York City to L.A., and halfway back again!

FACT 9 WE DON'T KNOW THE DEPTH OF THE CONGO

But we do know it's the deepest river in the world. Scientists have tried to measure it using equipment meant for the ocean, and think it is over 720 feet (220 m) deep. That's deeper than much of the Irish Sea!

Split personality

The Congo River is only the ninth-longest in the world, but in its lower reaches it is deep and fast. The river runs across central Africa, crossing the equator along the way. To begin with, it is a slow and winding river, but for the last 200 miles (320 km) it flows furiously with whirlpools and rapids. Its unique character makes it home to a huge number of endemic species (ones found nowhere else in the world).

Upper river

The Congo is unusual, as the upper section of a river, its "youthful" stage, is usually the steepest and fastest part, with lots of erosion. Water swirls around obstacles such as stones or rocks on the riverbed. It picks them up and they roll and bump along, cutting steep, narrow valleys as they go.

THE RIO NEGRO FLOWS ALONGSIDE THE AMAZON FOR 3.7 MILES (6 KM) WITHOUT THE DARK AND PALE WATERS MIXING.

Middle river

As a river slows it reaches its "mature" stage, winding across gentler landscapes. The course may bend dramatically in a series of S-shaped curves called meanders. The river erodes the outside edge of a bend and leaves deposits on the inside edge, rerouting the water until it eventually cuts off the corner, leaving an oxbow lake.

Erosion on the curves of a river can change its course.

Lower river

Two rivers, or tributaries, join at a point called the confluence. You can sometimes see this happening, such as when the Amazon and Negro Rivers meet (pictured below). Eventually, most rivers will reach their "old age," moving across flatter land and flowing slowly to the sea. A river always flows slightly downhill, even if it looks flat.

FACT 10

NIAGARA FALLS IS MOVING BACKWARD

There are three waterfalls at Niagara Falls, on the U.S.-Canadian border. So much water flows over their edges that the rock beneath is being worn away, and the falls are moving back up the river every year.

Breaking down

A waterfall forms where a river flows off a rocky ledge. When the falls occur over layers of rock with different hardnesses, the force of the water wears away both rocks, but the soft rock erodes much faster. It creates a plunge pool beneath, and the swirling action of the water breaks away more soft rock, creating an overhang. This may eventually break away, moving the waterfall back up the river.

NIAGARA FALLS IS THE WIDEST AND MOST POWERFUL WATERFALL IN NORTH AMERICA.

FACT 11

Enough electricity is made by the Niagara Falls power plants to power 3.8 million homes.

Moving fast

The Niagara River splits three ways at the falls, to flow around two small islands. It forms the Horseshoe Falls, named for its curving shape, the American Falls (on the U.S. side of the border), and the Bridal Veil Falls, the smallest of the three. The Horseshoe Falls used to erode so quickly that it moved backward over 3 feet (1 m) every year, but the flow of the river has been reduced so it now erodes around 1 foot (0.3 m) every 10 years.

Angel Falls is named after an aviator who crashed his plane at the top.

Use the power

Niagara Falls is an example of a block waterfall, where masses of water descend from a wide stream. The huge volumes of water are what make Niagara such an amazing sight. Some of the water can be diverted from the river above the falls to generate electricity in hydroelectric power stations. A series of gates are raised and lowered to channel the water to the stations, or allow it to flow directly over the falls.

Amazing falls

The world's highest waterfall is Angel Falls in the jungle of Venezuela. It is more than 15 times the height of Niagara Falls, tumbling off the edge of a flat-topped mountain called a tepui. The water falls so far that in the warm, dry season when the river's flow is reduced, the water evaporates before it touches the ground and forms a mist.

FACT 12 GLACIERS CAN BE EXPORTED!

The ice contained in glaciers can be tens of thousands of years old, and free of modern-day pollution. That makes it appealing to use as ice cubes in drinks, for drinking water, and for cutting large blocks to make beautiful sculptures.

Luxury ice

The governments of glacial areas such as Alaska and Greenland authorize the harvesting of ice from ancient glaciers. To reduce environmental impact, the ice is taken from sections that have already calved off the glacier. Large ice blocks are transported to be used in ice sculpting competitions around the world, and millions of ice cubes are sold to luxury hotels for their clarity, purity, and the fascinating crackle and pop they make as they melt!

Fitz Roy glacier is in the Patagonian mountains in South America.

Let it snow

A glacier is a river of ice, but it is not the same as a frozen river. Some free-flowing rivers may freeze over in winter, but a glacier is made entirely of snow that has fallen and frozen year after year. If the snow doesn't melt, it becomes compacted into an ice sheet. Most glaciers are found in mountain ranges, creeping slowly down and carving U-shaped valleys as they move.

FACT 13

There have been eight Ice Ages in the last 750,000 years.

Ice cycle

Lots of glaciers have been around since the last Ice Age, which ended around 11,500 years ago. During that time, polar ice extended from the North Pole to as far south as Great Britain and Ireland, Germany and Poland, and the midwestern U.S. An Ice Age, or glacial period, lasts for thousands of years, and is followed by a warmer period called an interglacial period.

Disappearing act

Glaciers are found around the world, from Peru and New Zealand to Canada and Russia. They even occur in hot countries such as Tanzania and Indonesia, high in the mountains. However, many glaciers are getting smaller, or retreating, as global temperatures rise. Scientists are concerned that the retreat rate is getting faster, and some of our most stunning glaciers might disappear in the next 20 years. Retreating glaciers affect mountain ecosystems, home to animals like the snow leopard.

FACT 14 SOME LAKES CAN EXPLODE!

Lake Nyos in Cameroon is one of a handful of lakes that contains so much carbon dioxide, it can explode. It has already destroyed homes and taken lives, and is still a potential danger.

LAKE BAIKAL IN RUSSIA CONTAINS MORE WATER THAN ALL OF THE U.S. GREAT LAKES PUT TOGETHER.

Dangerous waters

The bottom of Lake Nyos (pictured below) hides a layer of carbon dioxide which leaks into the water. When this is disturbed, it bubbles up and erupts. The explosion is not the only danger. The carbon dioxide that is released will suffocate local people unless they can get to higher ground. The boundaries of the lake are under permanent threat of breaking, which would cause flooding and a large-scale release of more carbon dioxide.

Beavers build dams that create ponds and lakes.

Glacier lakes

A glacier's movement can form a lake. As the ice pushes down a mountainside, it scrapes away a U-shaped basin and forces rocks and stones in front of it. If the glacier retreats or melts, these rocks form a natural barrier to hold water in long, narrow lakes. The Great Lakes in the U.S. and Canada are the largest examples in the world, and the Lake District (UK), lochs of Scotland, and fjord lakes of Norway are all stunning glacial creations.

Crater lakes

Lakes are a common occurrence on the tops of volcanic peaks. Lake Nyos is one example. A volcanic eruption leaves a crater, which forms a natural basin for a lake to form. Sometimes the whole magma chamber collapses, leaving a bigger crater called a caldera. This fills with rainwater or melted snow and ice to form a crystal-clear lake.

Make a lake!

There are millions of lakes on this planet. They are bodies of water surrounded by land, and are formed in various ways. Some are tiny and are known as ponds. Others are big enough to be called seas, such as the Caspian Sea, which is the largest in the world (although not the deepest, that is Lake Baikal). Both the Caspian Sea and Lake Baikal were formed by movements in Earth's crust, creating a natural dip in the rocks.

LAKE BOHINJ IN SLOVENIA IS A GLACIAL LAKE DAMMED BY ROCKS.

FACT 15 PREDJAMA CASTLE IS BUILT IN A CAVE

Caves can be found on the coast or in rock formations inland. The spectacular Predjama Castle in Slovenia is built partway up a cliff, in the mouth of a cavern, to help defend it from invaders.

GYPSUM IS A ROCK SO SOLUBLE THAT A TRUCK-SIZED BLOCK WOULD DISSOLVE IN 18 MONTHS IF PLACED IN A RIVER.

Going underground

Predjama Castle is located at the entrance to a whole network of caves and tunnels. It is typical of a karst landscape—an area of soft rocks that can be dissolved and eroded by water. Karst countryside has steep cliffs and underground passages and caverns, often with rivers running through them. You may also find sinkholes—large chasms where the surface rock has collapsed into the empty space beneath.

Dripping water contains dissolved limestone from the rocks.

Rock formations

Cave systems have their own unique interior design features. The best known are stalactites and stalagmites. Both are formed by the constant dripping of water from the cave roof. Minerals that have dissolved in the water collect to form solid trails hanging from the ceiling (stalactites), much like an icicle hanging down. Stalagmites grow upward from the floor as the minerals collect where the water drips.

Taking shelter

Caves provide natural shelter from the cold and rain. Cavemen weren't entirely stupid, you know! However, prehistoric cave dwellers had to share their space with bears and other wild animals, and were more likely to make their own shelters elsewhere. Even in the modern era, people descend into caves. They use them to hide during wartime, as an alternative to building houses, or to find a cool place away from the scorching desert heat.

On the beach

Coastal caves are created by the sea. The constant pounding of waves throws sand and stones at the cliff face, grinding away at small cracks and making them larger. Eventually the cracks open up into caves. On a headland, this may break right through to create an arch. A large arch may collapse, leaving a single pillar called a stack, sticking up on its own.

THE FRENCH COAST AT ÉTRETAT IS FAMOUS FOR ITS ARCHES AND WHITE CHALK CLIFFS.

EVEN MORE FACTS!

You've found out lots about mountains and rivers, but there's always more to discover! Boost your knowledge with these 10 quick facts.

Mount St. Helens, in the U.S. is an active volcano and type of volcanic mountain, formed when molten rock and ash erupts, piles on the surface, and builds a cone of rock.

The world's top five mountain peaks are: 1. Mount Everest, 29,028 ft (8,848 m); 2. K2, 28,251 ft (8,611 m); 3. Kanchenjunga, 28,205 ft (8,597 m); 4. Lhotse, Nepal 27,920 ft (8,510 m); 5. Makalu, 27,756 ft (8,460 m)

Mountain goats live in the mountains of North America. Their cloven hooves have two toes that spread wide to help them balance, and rough pads on the bottom of each toe help them grip.

The five longest mountain ranges in the world are: 1. The Andes, 4,350 miles (7,000 km); 2. Rocky Mountains, 2,980 miles (4,800 km); 3. Great Dividing Range, 2,300 miles (3,700 km); 4. Transantarctic Mountains, 2,175 miles (3,500 km); 5. Himalayas, 1,490 miles (2,400 km)

It's estimated that about 10 percent of the water vapor in the atmosphere comes from transpiration. The water is constantly replaced by a column of water moving up through the plant from its roots.

Scientists who study rivers and other freshwater bodies of water such as ponds and lakes are called limnologists.

The African lungfish lives in rivers in West Africa. In dry periods, when the river water levels are low, it burrows into the mud and surrounds itself in slime. For this dormant period, it uses a lung-like air bladder to breathe instead of its gills.

Angel Falls is named after the U.S. pilot Jimmie Angel, who was the first person to fly over the falls in 1933. Angel Falls is three times the height of the Eiffel Tower in Paris.

Glaciers that end in a body of water, such as a lake or an ocean, are called calving glaciers. This is from icebergs that break off the glacier, or "calve" into the water.

The Caspian Sea is the largest lake by surface area in the world. Five different countries have coastlines on the lake, including Russia, Iran, Kazakhstan, Azerbaijan, and Turkmenistan, and over 130 rivers flow into it.

MOUNTAINS AND RIVERS GLOSSARY

altitude A high place or region.

atmosphere The layer of air or other gases that surrounds a planet.

brackish Slightly salty water from marshes near the sea.

carbon dioxide One of the greenhouse gases in the atmosphere that cause global warming.

cirrus A type of thin, white cloud that forms at high altitudes.

condense To change from gas into liquid.

confluence The place where two rivers join to become one larger river.

contiguous U.S. The 48 adjoining states, plus the District of Columbia, on the continent of North America.

convergent Moving toward the same point.

cumulonimbus A dense, towering, vertical cloud, formed from powerful upward air currents.

delta An area of low, flat land, where a river splits and spreads out into several branches before entering the sea.

dormant Not active, but capable of becoming active later on.

ecosystem All the plants and animals that live in a particular area, along with the relationships between them and their environment.

endemic Frequently found in an area or region.

erosion The wearing away of rock or soil by rivers, the sea, or the weather.

estuary The wide part of a river, where it joins the sea.

evaporates Changes from a liquid to a gas state due to an increase in temperature.

faults Long cracks in the surface of the Earth that occur at plate boundaries, where earthquakes occur.

fertile Able to support the growth of a lot of strong, healthy plants.

fold mountains Mountains that form by the effects of folding on layers of Earth's crust.

geyser A hole in Earth's surface from which hot water and steam are forced out.

hydroelectric Involving electricity made from the energy of running water.

Ice Age A period of time lasting many thousands of years, during which a lot of Earth's surface was covered with ice.

icebergs Large, tall masses of ice floating in the sea.

ice sheets Large, thick areas of ice, especially those that have existed for a long time.

inhabited Lived in.

irrigation Supplying water to crops on farmland.

magma Molten rock that is formed in very hot conditions inside Earth.

manufacturing The business of making things in factories.

millennia Periods of 1,000 years.

oxbow lake A small, curved lake on the flood plain of a river formed from part of the river in the past.

MOUNTAINS AND RIVERS GLOSSARY continued

plates Pieces of Earth's lithosphere, made up of the crust and upper part of the mantle.

prohibited Banned.

rapids A section of a river where the water moves very fast, often over rocks.

red blood cells Blood cells of vertebrate animals that carry oxygen and carbon dioxide to and from the body's tissues.

sanitation Keeping places clean and healthy, especially by providing a sewage system and a clean water supply.

source Where a river or stream begins.

species A class of plants or animals that share the same main characteristics and are able to breed with each other.

summit Another word for peak, or top of a mountain.

tide The regular change in the level of the sea on the shore.

transpiration The evaporation of water from a plant's leaves, stem, or flowers.

tributaries Streams or rivers that flow into a larger one.

whirlpool A small area in a river or the sea, where the water is moving quickly in a circular direction so that objects floating near it are pulled into its center.

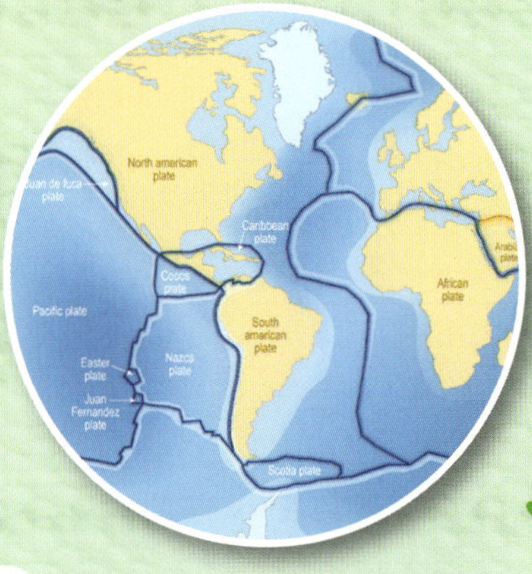

FURTHER INFORMATION

BOOKS

Brake, Mark. *The Big Earth Book*. London, UK: Lonely Planet Kids, 2017.

Cullis, Megan. *The Usborne Book of Planet Earth*. London, UK: Usborne, 2019.

DK. *DKfindout! Earth*. London, UK: DK, 2017.

DK. *Earth: The Definitive Visual Guide*. London, UK: DK, 2013.

DK. *Pocket Eyewitness Earth: Facts at Your Fingertips*. London, UK: DK, 2018.

Gallagher, Belinda. *Wild About Planet Earth*. Thaxted, UK: Miles Kelly, 2019.

MacDonald, Fiona, and Rupert Matthews. *100 Facts Extreme Earth*. Thaxted, UK: Miles Kelly, 2017.

WEBSITES

CoolKidFacts
https://www.coolkidfacts.com/earth-science/
Discover all sorts of facts about planet Earth, from deserts and mountains to the different types of rocks on our planet. Includes simple science experiments and activity worksheets.

Ducksters Earth Science for Kids
https://www.ducksters.com/science/earth_science/
Head to this website to find out all there is to know about planet Earth; you can also try an earth science crossword puzzle and word search!

Science4Fun
http://science4fun.info/earth-science/
Find out more about planet Earth's geology, meteorology, paleontolog,y and oceanography.

Publisher's note to educators and parents: Our editors have carefully reviewed these websites to ensure that they are suitable for students. Many websites change frequently, however, and we cannot guarantee that a site's future contents will continue to meet our high standards of quality and educational value. Be advised that students should be closely supervised whenever they access the Internet.

INDEX